TONY HAWK

BY RAYMOND H. MILLER

KIDHAVEN
PRESS™

THOMSON
_____✦_____ ™
GALE

San Diego • Detroit • New York • San Francisco • Cleveland
New Haven, Conn. • Waterville, Maine • London • Munich

© 2004 by KidHaven Press. KidHaven Press is an imprint of The Gale Group, Inc., a division of Thomson Learning, Inc.

KidHaven™ and Thomson Learning™ are trademarks used herein under license.

For more information, contact
KidHaven Press
27500 Drake Rd.
Farmington Hills, MI 48331-3535
Or you can visit our Internet site at http://www.gale.com

LIBRARY OF CONGRESS CATALOGING-IN-PUBLICATION DATA

Miller, Raymond H., 1967-
  Tony Hawk / by Raymond H. Miller.
    v. cm. — (Stars of sport)
  Includes bibliographical references.
  Contents: Introduction: Man on a mission—Wild child—Dogtown days—Big air—A skateboarding phenomenon.
    ISBN 0-7377-1568-5
  1. Hawk, Tony—Juvenile literature. 2. Skateboarders—United States—Biography—Juvenile literature. [1. Hawk, Tony. 2. Skateboarders.] I. Title. II. Series.
  GV859.813.H39M55 2004
  796.22'092—dc22

                                                              2003023376

Printed in the United States of America

Contents

Man on a Mission

Tony Hawk learned to ride a skateboard at the age of nine. Remarkably, he began skating professionally just five years later. This happened in the early 1980s, when skateboarding was considered more of a hobby than a sport. Those who skated were not thought of as athletes. Most of the time they were seen as misfits and outcasts. But Hawk slowly began to change those perceptions. He loved riding the steep ramps of **vertical (vert) skating,** and he invented his own aerial tricks at southern California's skate parks. Other skateboarders at first made fun of his odd-looking maneuvers. In time, though, they came to recognize him as one of the most creative and talented skaters in the sport.

Tony Hawk started skateboarding at the age of nine and today he is one of the world's most talented skaters.

Skateboarding rose and fell in popularity several times in the 1980s and 1990s, but Hawk stayed with the sport and kept improving. He won more than fifty competitions to rule vert skating. It was not until 1999 that he became an international phenomenon. This marked the first time he landed the extremely difficult 900, a trick in which he spun two and a half times in midair before landing on his skateboard.

Although Hawk has since retired from competitive skateboarding, he has stayed active in the sport. He owns a successful skateboard company and frequently performs in exhibitions around the country. He also remains the sport's most popular skater. Tony Hawk will forever be known as the person who turned a hobby for outsiders into a sport for the masses.

Wild Child

Anthony ("Tony") Frank Hawk was born on May 12, 1968, in San Diego, California. He was much younger than Frank and Marilyn Hawk's other three children. Tony's sister Lenore was twenty-one when he was born, while sister Patricia was eighteen and brother Steve was twelve. Frank Hawk, age forty-five when Tony was born, was a decorated navy pilot. He had received numerous air medals for his achievements during World War II and the Korean War. Long since retired from the military, Frank worked as a salesman until he was laid off just before Tony was born. He then moved from job to job to support his family. Marilyn Hawk also worked, but she went back to college to earn her degree at age thirty-seven, five years

Tony Hawk, seen here signing autographs, is the youngest of four Hawk children.

before Tony was born. She returned to work when Tony was a toddler to supplement Frank's income.

As the baby of the family, Tony often pushed the limits of bad behavior. He frequently threw objects from his crib at the nanny, sometimes hitting her. After several months of dealing with his behavior problems, the nanny quit. Marilyn later tried enrolling Tony in a preschool near their home in Serra Mesa, California, but he resisted. Each morning he kicked and screamed as his father pulled him from the car to the preschool entrance. Then he ran to the chain-link fence and cried as his father drove away. Tony was at the preschool for only a few months when his teachers expelled him for bad behavior.

Ahead of the Class

Tony's tantrums grew worse. If the family was playing Scrabble® and he saw that he was going to lose, he would overturn the game board so that nobody could win. At age five, his mother tried to teach him how to play tennis. The game was too slow paced for him. When she gently lobbed the ball over the net, he slammed the balls directly back at her. Another time, she took him to an Olympic-sized pool to swim. Not satisfied with swimming in the shallow end, he spent the whole time trying to swim the length of the pool underwater. When he failed, he left in anger.

Despite the tantrums, Tony was a fast learner. By the time he reached kindergarten, he already knew how to read. He wanted to keep learning, so he began reading from the next grade's textbooks. He also knew how to count and subtract numbers quickly, something the other students could not yet do.

When Tony was in second grade, he became distracted and bored with basic math, a subject he already knew well. The school board considered moving him up a grade, where he would be more challenged. But Tony's parents decided against the idea, fearing he might not fit in with the older students.

A New Love

Tony began playing organized basketball and Little
League baseball. He played both sports with reckless
abandon. In basketball he was out of control, running ag-
gressively after loose balls. He even broke his finger once
while diving to the floor. In Tony's first time up to bat in
Little League, he hit a single and beamed with joy while
standing on first base. He hated experiencing failure of
any kind, though. When he struck out in his next at bat,
he ran and hid in a ravine on the other side of the field.

Tony continued to play both sports, but at age nine
he began skateboarding when his brother, Steve, gave
him an old fiberglass "banana board." The two went to a
nearby alley, and Steve taught Tony the basics of skateboarding. Tony rolled down the alley until he ran out of
speed. Then he got off the board, turned it around, got
back on, and started over. Next Tony learned how to
carve and kickturn so he could stay on the board instead
of always jumping off and back on.

"I wouldn't say when I first started I was a natural by
any means," Tony recalled. "But I kind of liked trying
things out, the process of learning something new but
not having to follow a practice schedule or rely on other
people to make it happen. That was really what the draw
was for me."[1]

Skating Oasis

When Tony was in fourth grade, he and his friends
started riding their skateboards around the neighbor-
hood streets after school. Tony became bored with the

Tony Hawk learned to skate on a fiberglass board similar to the boards used by the skaters in this 1965 photo.

flat surface. He pleaded for his parents to take him to nearby Oasis Skate Park, a popular skateboarding facility. Oasis had two empty swimming pools, a **half-pipe**, and other sloped surfaces that fascinated Tony. Instead, Frank built a small ramp for Tony to do jumps and kick-turns in the driveway.

After Tony became bored with skating on streets, he began to ride the half-pipes at the local skate park.

The next year Tony finally made it to Oasis. He quickly put on his helmet and ankle, knee, and wrist pads and hopped on his skateboard. He skated all day, rarely stopping for a break. Before long he was spending all of his free time at Oasis, and the hard work was paying off. By age eleven he was one of the youngest but best skaters at the skate park.

As Tony's love for skating grew, his interest in baseball and basketball faded. One day he was skating at
Oasis when his father came to pick him up for basketball practice. "I wanted to stay at the park even longer,"
he recalled. "But I had to run to practice. I was still
wearing my knee pads when I got to the gym! [That
night] I told my dad, 'I don't want to play other sports
anymore. I just want to skateboard.'"[2] His father gave his
approval and the decision officially ended Tony's days of
playing team sports.

Dogtown Days

By the early 1980s skateboarding had evolved from the casual "sidewalk surfing" style of the 1960s to a more radical sport. It involved athletic and sometimes dangerous tricks. Tony started slowly, first learning 180-degree turns called **rock 'n' rolls.** These helped him learn balance, an important part of skating the half-pipe. Next he worked up the courage to try aerials, or **airs**, by propelling himself into the air at the top of the ramp. Then he tried **fakies**, where he came back down the ramp backward instead of turning around and facing forward. Tony fell, or **slammed**, constantly as he practiced the maneuvers, collecting an assortment of broken teeth, bruises, and cuts in the process.

Watching the other skaters at Oasis was helpful to Tony. He studied their moves, such as grabbing the nose of the skateboard during airs, a trick his idol, Eddie Elguera, mastered. Then he put the moves into practice and would not be satisfied until he could perform them. Despite all the practice, Tony was not fully prepared when he entered his first competition at age eleven. He

Tony practices a high-speed grind on the lip of a half-pipe.

Tony performs a trick during an exhibition in Toronto, Canada. As a young skater, Tony often felt nervous when he competed in front of crowds.

was extremely nervous skating in front of a crowd and fell on most of his tricks. He finished near the bottom of his age group. He was crushed.

Tony was disappointed in his error-filled performance, but he did not let it dampen his enthusiasm for the sport. He was determined to eliminate the mistakes and spent even more practice time at Oasis. Eventually Tony was able to do an advanced trick called a **frontside** rock 'n' roll, which few other skaters were able to perform. In fact, the judges moved Tony up a level because he was landing the trick with ease. By the end of his first year of competition, he was finishing at or near the top of his age group.

Supportive Family

Tony's parents took an active part in his budding skateboarding career. Frank not only drove Tony to Oasis several times a week, but also attended Tony's competitions all around southern California. The Hawks regularly invited as many as twenty out-of-town skaters to stay at their home during weekend contests at Oasis. One of the overnight visitors, the manager of the Dogtown Skateboards team, was impressed with Tony's ability. She eventually offered him a place on the team, which he quickly accepted. Being on a skateboarding team at that time amounted to little more than free **decks, trucks,** and wheels, the main parts of a skateboard. But with some of the top skaters in southern California on the Dogtown team, it was an incredible honor for someone as young as Tony to be a member.

Just after Tony joined Dogtown and was seen as a rising star in the sport, skateboarding was fading fast in popularity. With the exception of Oasis and a few others, skate parks were going out of business. The Association of Skatepark Owners also came to an end, leaving no official body to organize competitions. Frank Hawk immediately stepped in. He helped create the California Amateur Skateboard League (CASL) and later started the National Skateboarding Association (NSA). He and several others at CASL organized skateboarding competitions in the area while Tony's mother kept score at the events.

Turning Point

In school, Tony continued to receive good grades even though his life totally revolved around skateboarding. His clothes had holes and his body was covered with bruises and scabs from slamming on the vert ramp. When Tony's seventh-grade teacher let each student take a turn teaching the class about the subject of his or her choice, he naturally chose skateboarding. As part of the lesson, Tony's father brought a projector to school so Tony could play a film of himself doing tricks at Oasis. But skateboarding was considered a dead fad, and the other students teased him for continuing to participate in it.

At the end of seventh grade, Tony and his family moved to Cardiff, California. He was happy to move, because their new home was just a five-minute drive to Del Mar Surf and Turf, another skate park that had remained open despite a lack of skaters.

Around that time, Dogtown went out of business, and Tony was without a team. One of his skateboarding heroes, Stacy Peralta, saw him skate at a competition and was impressed. Peralta, a skating champion in the 1970s, was known for being a good judge of talent. He had discovered the likes of Steve Caballero and Mike McGill, two skaters who were known for their amazing aerial tricks. Tony greatly admired all three skaters. So, he was honored when Peralta offered him a spot on his Powell Peralta Skateboards team, nicknamed the Bones Brigade. A few months before his thirteenth birthday, Tony joined Peralta's team.

Tony slides down a half-pipe wall on his kneepads. At first, Tony often returned from competitions battered and bruised after crashing on the half-pipe.

The Bones Brigade

Because of his age, Tony was still competing as an amateur when he started with Powell Peralta Skateboards. He had only ever skated against regional competition. In 1981 he got his first taste of national competition when the team flew to Jacksonville, Florida, for a national vert contest. Tony skated terribly in all his runs in Jacksonville and missed the finals. He hardly spoke the entire trip back to California.

Once home, Tony went back to practice and vowed to do better. His main problem was a lack of confidence. Most of the skaters on the team were several years older than Tony and had competed in dozens of contests. They were comfortable skating in front of crowds and competing against better skaters. Tony had little experience at the national level and his nervousness affected his skating.

Over the next two years, Tony skated with the Bones Brigade, developed confidence, and learned how to prepare for competition from his older teammates. He won most of the amateur vert contests he entered, both regional and national. He also performed well skating the curbs, benches, and handrails of **street style** competitions.

A few months after Tony's fourteenth birthday, Peralta approached him before a contest and asked if he wanted to turn pro. It was a big step for someone Tony's age. Most of the professionals were eighteen and older. He thought about it, filled out the contest registration form, and checked the "pro" box.

Tony was officially a professional skateboarder. He skated much better in his professional debut than he had as an amateur. He won a trophy for third place but received no money. Skateboarding contests during that time were struggling to survive and no longer awarded cash prizes. The sport was still highly unpopular. Perhaps that is why the move to pro did not overly excite him. "I can't remember being super-hyped that day and jumping around with a massive smile stuck to my face," he recalled. "When I told my parents I had turned pro they said, 'That's nice.'"[3]

Big Air

It was fitting that Tony had joined a team called the Bones Brigade. At age fourteen, he weighed just eighty pounds, and his skinny arms and legs poked out of his safety equipment in a comical way. Because he was so light, he had problems gaining the speed necessary for **big airs** at the top of the vert ramp. To solve that problem, he became the first skater to lead into tricks by doing an **ollie**, a move in which he became airborne by tapping the tail of the board on the ground and springing upward. He then grabbed the board and held it beneath his feet while turning or spinning in midair. Veteran skaters teased him for the awkward move, but it allowed him to keep improving. Hawk's signature move would eventually catch on with other skaters and become a key part of nearly every trick in vert skating.

The following year Hawk added height and weight and became stronger as a result. The added power on the vert ramp finally gave him the ability and the confidence to execute big airs. Peralta was amazed at Tony's rapid progress and his maturity. At age fifteen, he took first place in just his second pro competition, but he was never overly concerned about where he placed in competition. His appearance on the cover of *Thrasher*, a popular skateboarding magazine, was more gratifying to him than any trophy he had won to that point.

Reaping the Rewards

In the early to mid-1980s the appeal of vert skating, with its speed and big air elements, was growing. Tony still competed in street contests, but vert was his strength, and he soon got to show the world what he could do. The Bones Brigade traveled to Australia, Canada, Europe, and throughout much of the United States giving demonstrations. Hawk and his teammates were treated like superstars and had to fend off admiring but rowdy teenagers.

Hawk was also becoming a major marketing star in the skateboarding world. He had a Powell professional skateboard named after him and received a small amount of money for every board that sold. Powell also produced Hawk posters, stickers, and T-shirts. In 1983 Tony Hawk was earning between five hundred dollars

Tony grabs his board as he completes a difficult aerial spin during a competition in Melbourne, Australia, in 2002.

and one thousand dollars a month from the sales of his products. The next year he appeared in the *Bones Brigade Video Show*, a movie that featured the team doing various tricks and stunts. The video was enormously popular. Money from video sales increased Hawk's monthly income by three thousand dollars.

But Hawk was not skating for the money. His goal was to become one of the sport's greatest champions, and he was not far from reaching it. In competition he regularly landed the 540—one and a half rotations with a flip in the middle. Then he dazzled crowds by making another half rotation to complete the difficult 720. At a competition in France he tried another half turn for what many people thought was an impossible trick—the 900. He came up short and slammed, fracturing a rib. The crash made him all the more determined to land the difficult trick someday.

Brief Retirement

By 1986 skateboarding was booming, thanks to the exposure from the Bones Brigade video. Hawk was at the top of the sport, winning almost every top competition he entered. At one point he won three contests in a row, a feat no professional skater had ever accomplished. Because he was so focused on skateboarding, his grades slipped to a C average his senior year in high school. But by then he had decided to skip college to continue his career in skateboarding. His parents supported his decision to stick with the sport he loved. By age nineteen, he was earning more than $150,000 dollars a year from video sales, sponsorships, and contest winnings.

But with success came criticism. Many people in the skateboarding community still disliked Hawk's style, calling him too stiff and robotic. People also began to say

Tony flips upside down as he performs a 540, a difficult trick involving one and a half rotations with a flip in the middle.

that if he finished anywhere but in first place, he had failed. That bothered Hawk because he only wanted to meet the standards he had set for himself and not worry about the judges' opinions. He became depressed and withdrew from the skating scene. "I grew sick of skating in contests and having people only pay attention to how I placed. It got to be so mundane—not for me necessarily, but for everyone else involved. I'd had enough."[4] Before his twentieth birthday, and not yet at the height of his career, he retired from competitive skateboarding.

Tony spins through a grab at the 2003 X Games. Despite Tony's tremendous success, some skaters have criticized his style as stiff and robotic.

In the meantime, Hawk bought a house in Fallbrook, California, and together with his father built a thirty-thousand-dollar skateboard ramp in the backyard. He skated the ramp frequently to stay in shape, but he also spent time relaxing with friends. After three months away from competitive skating, he had a new attitude and was ready to return to the skating circuit. In his first event back he finished second, but before long he was ranked number one in the world again after winning titles in Denmark and Germany.

Birdhouse Projects

In 1990 Hawk married Cindy Dunbar, a woman he had dated on and off for several years. The two had a son, Riley, in 1992. With his personal life in order and his skating career back on track, Hawk was ready to move ahead. However, skateboarding had fallen into another slump. By the summer of 1990, the NSA was in financial trouble and fewer competitions were being held. When the Bones Brigade went on the road, they performed in front of crowds of less than fifty people. With Hawk's income decreasing each month, the future looked bleak. That was when he decided to take control of his career. He left Powell, took out a second mortgage on his house, and with forty thousand dollars started Birdhouse Projects.

The new company promoted Tony Hawk signature skateboards and clothing. It also sponsored a skating team that Hawk had put together personally. But with the skateboarding market in collapse and Birdhouse

To help promote his line of clothing and skateboards, Tony often skated without pay at exhibitions like this one in South Africa.

struggling to survive, he could barely afford to pay the skaters. To promote Birdhouse Projects, the team skated in exhibitions throughout the Midwest and on the East Coast. It was a low-budget tour. They skated in front of small crowds, sometimes for free, and slept five to a room. "By the time I drove the van back to Birdhouse's small office, we'd lost $7,000," Hawk said. "We knew we'd lose money, but it was our investment in the future—we hoped."[5]

By 1994 Hawk considered closing the business because it cost more to keep it open than it was making. At home things were even more troubled. Tony and Cindy's marriage was falling apart, and Riley was not yet one year old. In September of that year the two separated, and several months later they divorced. It marked a low point in Hawk's life.

A Skateboarding Phenomenon

With Hawk's personal and professional life in turmoil, the talented skater retired from competition again. But he did not quit skating entirely. He practiced on his vert ramp at Fallbrook and at the local YMCA, where he continued to invent new tricks. The **heelflip varial lien** was a particularly hard trick to learn, because he had to kick the board with his heel so the board flipped and turned 180 degrees before he caught it in midair and landed on it. After about thirty tries he finally landed one. Accomplishing such a difficult trick gave him reason to believe for the first time in a year that he was still able to improve as a skater.

At the same time, skateboarding was slowly making a comeback. Birdhouse Projects' summer tour schedule included amusement parks, state fairs, and skate parks around the country. In the spring of 1995, Hawk joined Extreme Wheels Live, a family-type show in Santa Rosa, California, that mixed BMX bicycle racing, in-line skating, and skateboarding. He was one of the featured skateboarders in the show, and crowds turned out in large numbers to see him. It was there that he met Erin, an in-line skater in the show who was paying her way through college. The two dated for about a year, then married in September 1996. They later had two sons, Spencer and Keegan.

Throughout his career, Tony has invented several complicated skating tricks, including the heelflip varial lien (pictured), a difficult trick performed in midair.

Going to Extremes

In 1995 skateboarding was in the midst of another comeback. Hawk decided Birdhouse Projects could benefit from the growing interest in the sport if he started skating in contests again. So in June of that year he competed in the first ESPN Extreme Games (later called the X Games), an Olympic-style event that featured BMX racing, in-line skating, skateboarding, and other extreme sports. Hawk placed first in the vert contest and second in street competition. Millions of television viewers witnessed Hawk's stunning aerial tricks on the vert ramp, including a 720, on his way to the gold medal.

By the mid-1990s, Tony's career as a professional skater was soaring and his clothing line and professional model skateboards were selling very well.

Hawk had long been famous in the skateboarding community, but after the X Games even nonskaters recognized him. Birdhouse Projects sales shot up as a result of his national exposure on ESPN, and Airwalk produced a Tony Hawk signature shoe that became the company's best seller.

With Hawk's career at an all-time high and his company about to take the skateboard market by storm, he received devastating news. His father, who had earlier been diagnosed with cancer, died during the summer of 1995 while Tony was on a skating tour with Birdhouse Projects. He took the death hard and immediately went to be with his mother. The family held a wake, which was attended by the dozens of skaters Frank had befriended through the years.

Nailing the 900

Hawk decided the best way to honor his father would be to return to skating. A few months later at a YMCA contest, he won all three categories: Highest Air, Highest Air to Fakie, and the Vert contest. At age twenty-seven, Hawk was firmly at the top of a sport that he had helped make more popular than ever with his electrifying ability. With Birdhouse Projects finally making money, Hawk bought a warehouse in Irvine, California, and built a huge ramp. He called the facility Birdland and spent hours there practicing when he was not on the road.

Birdhouse Projects continued to grow. By 1996 Hawk was overwhelmed with the responsibilities of running the business and organizing his skating schedule. His

Tony Hawk's Complete X Games History

Year	Discipline	Finish	Medal
*Summer 2003	Vert Best Trick	1	Gold
Summer 2002	Vert Best Trick	3	Bronze
Summer 2002	Vert Doubles	1	Gold
Summer 2001	Vert Best Trick	2	Silver
Summer 2001	Vert Doubles	1	Gold
Summer 2000	Vert Doubles	1	Gold
Summer 1999	Vert	3	Bronze
Summer 1999	Vert Best Trick	1	Gold
Summer 1999	Vert Doubles	1	Gold
Summer 1998	Vert	3	Bronze
Summer 1998	Vert Doubles	1	Gold
Summer 1997	Vert	1	Gold
Summer 1997	Vert Doubles	1	Gold
Summer 1996	Park	7	na
Summer 1996	Vert	2	Silver
Summer 1995	Park	2	Silver
Summer 1995	Vert	1	Gold

*Tony Hawk announced his retirement from X Games competition following his victory.

sister Pat, who had earlier worked in the entertainment industry, began to manage business arrangements for him so he could concentrate on skating.

The buildup to the second X Games was intense. ESPN was using Hawk's name and image to promote the X Games, and the pressure was squarely on him. He skated well during his runs but was edged out of first place. He came back the next year determined to recapture his title. After completing his first two runs nearly flawlessly, he attempted the 900 on his third and final run. He was unsuccessful, but still took the gold medal in vert. Two years later at the X Games, he tried the 900 again. This time he timed his air perfectly, spun two and a half times, and stayed on the board during his landing. The other skaters immediately swarmed around him as the crowd went wild. He had finally landed the trick that had frustrated him for so long, and it completed a list of tricks that he had made for himself a decade earlier.

Boom Boom HuckJam

The 900 did more than win Hawk another gold medal. It made him an international superstar. Highlights of the trick were shown on televisions around the world. He began receiving national endorsement deals that were once only available to baseball, basketball, and football stars. It became nearly impossible to satisfy all the requests for interviews and photo shoots.

At the end of 1999 Hawk landed another 900 to win Best Trick at an MTV-sponsored event in Las Vegas, Nevada. After that he reduced his competitive skating schedule to concentrate on Birdhouse Projects, which had become one of the nation's top skateboard sellers. In 2002 he also started Boom Boom HuckJam, a noncompetitive event that mixed skateboarding, freestyle BMX, and freestyle motocross with live rock performances. Children and adults packed into arenas around the country just to see their favorite skater in action.

Hawk also helped develop Activision's Tony Hawk Pro Skater series, which has been among the most popular video game series of all time. Partly because of the popularity of the video game series, Hawk was named favorite male athlete at the Nickelodeon Kids' Choice Awards in 2001. In 2002 he was voted "coolest big-time athlete" in an online poll for kids conducted by the youth marketing firm Alloy. He finished ahead of Tiger Woods, Michael Jordan, and Derek Jeter.

In addition to running Birdhouse Projects and touring with Boom Boom HuckJam, Hawk also devotes time to his Tony Hawk Foundation. The foundation donates more than four hundred thousand dollars a year to promote and build public skate parks around the country, often in low-income neighborhoods. For example, the city of Fort Wayne, Indiana, received a twenty-five-

Activision's Tony Hawk Pro Skater series is among the most popular video game series of all time.

Tony poses with his wife Karen and son Keegan. Although Tony now devotes most of his time to his family, he continues to skate as much as possible.

thousand-dollar grant from Hawk's foundation to build a skate park so a new generation of skateboarders there could enjoy the sport.

In 2003 Tony returned to the X Games and won Vert Best Trick after landing another 900, then announced his retirement once again. Now in his mid-thirties, Hawk wants to spend more time with his family. He explains why he keeps coming back to the sport that, like him, has gone through many ups and downs: "Skateboarding is my form of exercise, my sport, my means of expression since I was nine years old. It's what I love. I never expected it to give me anything more than that."[6]

Skateboard Tricks Invented by Tony Hawk

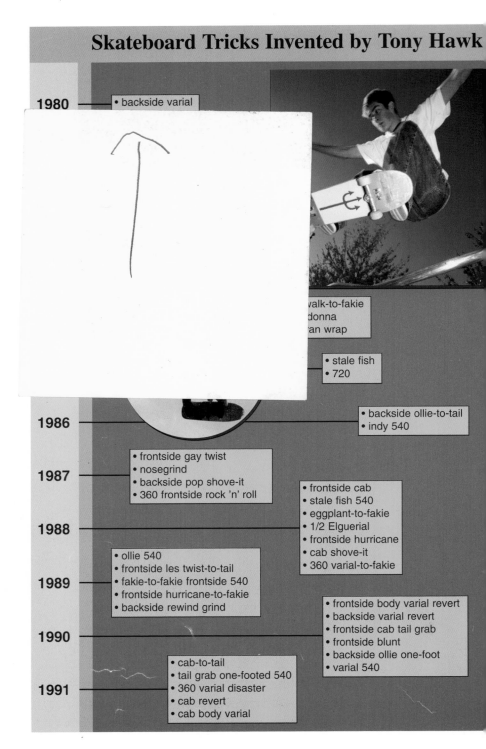

1980 — • backside varial

• walk-to-fakie
• madonna
• an wrap

• stale fish
• 720

1986 —
• backside ollie-to-tail
• indy 540

1987 —
• frontside gay twist
• nosegrind
• backside pop shove-it
• 360 frontside rock 'n' roll

• frontside cab
• stale fish 540
• eggplant-to-fakie
1988 —
• 1/2 Elguerial
• frontside hurricane
• cab shove-it
• 360 varial-to-fakie

• ollie 540
• frontside les twist-to-tail
1989 —
• fakie-to-fakie frontside 540
• frontside hurricane-to-fakie
• backside rewind grind

• frontside body varial revert
• backside varial revert
• frontside cab tail grab
1990 —
• frontside blunt
• backside ollie one-foot
• varial 540

• cab-to-tail
• tail grab one-footed 540
1991 —
• 360 varial disaster
• cab revert
• cab body varial

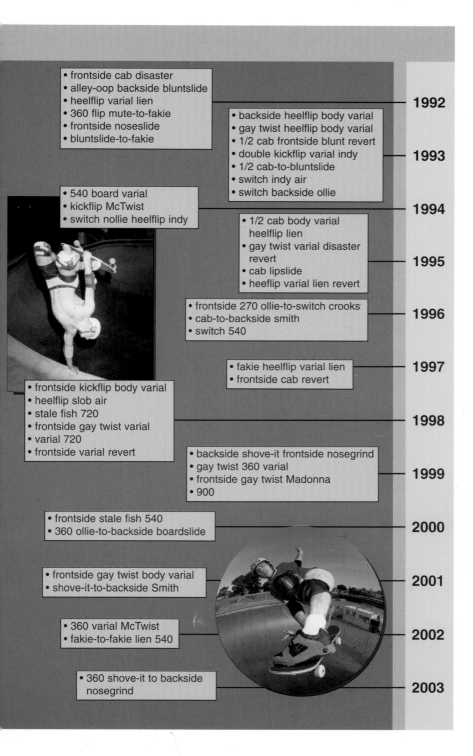

- frontside cab disaster
- alley-oop backside bluntslide
- heelflip varial lien
- 360 flip mute-to-fakie
- frontside noseslide
- bluntslide-to-fakie

1992

- backside heelflip body varial
- gay twist heelflip body varial
- 1/2 cab frontside blunt revert
- double kickflip varial indy
- 1/2 cab-to-bluntslide
- switch indy air
- switch backside ollie

1993

- 540 board varial
- kickflip McTwist
- switch nollie heelflip indy

1994

- 1/2 cab body varial heelflip lien
- gay twist varial disaster revert
- cab lipslide
- heeflip varial lien revert

1995

- frontside 270 ollie-to-switch crooks
- cab-to-backside smith
- switch 540

1996

- fakie heelflip varial lien
- frontside cab revert

1997

- frontside kickflip body varial
- heelflip slob air
- stale fish 720
- frontside gay twist varial
- varial 720
- frontside varial revert

1998

- backside shove-it frontside nosegrind
- gay twist 360 varial
- frontside gay twist Madonna
- 900

1999

- frontside stale fish 540
- 360 ollie-to-backside boardslide

2000

- frontside gay twist body varial
- shove-it-to-backside Smith

2001

- 360 varial McTwist
- fakie-to-fakie lien 540

2002

- 360 shove-it to backside nosegrind

2003

Notes

Chapter One: Wild Child

1. Quoted in John Rogers, "Tony Hawk Taking Kids' TV by Storm," AP Online, August 29, 2001. www.hollandsentinel.com/stories.

2. Quoted in Sean Mortimer, "Chairman of the Board: Meet Tony Hawk. His Job Is Skateboarding, and Nobody Does It Better!" *Sports Illustrated for Kids*, July 1, 1998, p. 62.

Chapter Two: Dogtown Days

3. Tony Hawk and Sean Mortimer, *Tony Hawk—Occupation: Skateboarder*. New York: Regan Books, 2000, p. 61.

Chapter Three: Big Air

4. Hawk and Mortimer, *Tony Hawk*, p. 133.

5. Hawk and Mortimer, *Tony Hawk*, p. 176.

Chapter Four: A Skateboarding Phenomenon

6. Quoted in Tim Layden, "What Is This Thirty-Four-Year-Old Man Doing on a Skateboard? Making Millions," *Sports Illustrated*, June 10, 2002, p. 80.

Glossary

air: Any maneuver in which all four wheels of the skateboard are off the ground at the same time.

big air: A trick in which a skateboarder launches his or her body and skateboard high above a vert ramp.

carve: To skate in long, curving patterns.

deck: The top surface of a skateboard.

fakie: Skating backward while standing on the board in the normal position.

frontside: A trick or maneuver in which the skater turns in the direction that his or her feet are facing.

half-pipe: A U-shaped ramp with a flat surface in the middle that is used in vertical skating. It allows a skater to ride down one side and up the other.

heelflip varial lien: A trick in which a skater flips the heel side of the board with his front foot, rotating it 180 degrees vertically, then grabs the board and places it back under his feet during an air.

kickturn: A turn made by lifting the front wheels of the skateboard off the ground by applying pressure to the tail of the board.

ollie: A move in which the skater taps the tail of the board on the ground to become airborne.

rock 'n' roll: A 180-degree turn at the top of a ramp or other vertical surface.

slam: A hard crash.

street style: A skating style in which skaters incorporate elements of urban landscapes into their routines.

truck: The front and rear axles that hold the wheels and are mounted to the deck.

vertical (vert) skating: Skating that takes place on ramps and other vertical surfaces.

For Further Exploration

Books

Michael Boughn and Joseph Romain, *Tony Hawk*. Toronto, Canada: Warwick, 2001. Provides a detailed look at Hawk's life and career as he rose from struggling amateur to world champion.

Matt Christopher, *On the Halfpipe with Tony Hawk*. New York: Little, Brown, 2001. Examines the life and career of the electrifying skateboarder.

Tony Hawk, *Between Boardslides and Burnout: My Notes from the Road*. New York: Regan Books, 2002. Hawk gives a firsthand account of what it is like being a professional skateboarder on the road. With photographs.

Tony Hawk and Sean Mortimer, *Tony Hawk: Professional Skateboarder*. New York: Regan Books, 2002. The skateboarding superstar shares stories about his family, childhood, and skating career.

Internet Source

EXPN.com, "Athlete Bio: Tony Hawk." http://expn. go.com. Provides a detailed look at Hawk's X Games record, with video clips of the skater performing tricks.

Website

Tony Hawk's Official Web Site (www.tonyhawk.com). Includes a biography, photo and video links, a road journal, and more.

Index

Picture Credits

Cover: © Duomo/CORBIS

AP/Wide World Photos, 15, 16, 39 (bottom)

© Bettmann/CORBIS, 11

Bloomberg News/Landov, 36

© Steve Boyle/NewSport/CORBIS, 32

© Corel Corporation, 39 (top)

© Matt A. Brown/X Games IX/NewSport/CORBIS, 19, 26

© Duomo/CORBIS, 5, 12, 31

© Photos.com, 38 (both)

© Rick Rickman/NewSport/CORBIS, 8, 25

Pierre Tostee/REUTERS/Landov, 23, 28

© Frank Trapper/CORBIS, 37

About the
Author

Raymond H. Miller is the author of more than fifty non-fiction books for children. He has written on a range of topics, from sports trivia to satellite surveillance. He enjoys playing sports and spending time outdoors with his wife and two daughters.

DATE			